Flight of the Butterflies

by Roberta Edwards

illustrated by Bob Kayganich
and with photographs

Grosset & Dunlap
An Imprint of Penguin Group (USA) Inc.

Most animals live

in one place

all their lives.

They never travel

far away.

This beaver lives

in the same stream

all its life.

This frog lives

in the same pond

all its life.

This tiger lives

in the same jungle

all its life.

But some animals live part of the year

in one place

and part of the year

in another place.

They make the same round trip

year after year.

This kind of trip is called migration
(say: my-GRAY-shun).
Every fall, Canada geese fly south
for the winter.
Some go as far as Mexico.
It is a long, hard trip.
But Canada geese are big and strong.

Every winter,

humpback whales swim thousands

of miles to warm tropical waters.

It is a long, hard trip.

But humpback whales are

big and strong.

Monarch butterflies are not

big or strong.

Yet at the end of the summer,

they begin

a long, hard trip, too.

ROCKY MOUNTAINS

MONARCH BUTTERFLIES

MEXICO

They cannot
survive cold winters.
So west of the Rockies,
monarchs fly to California.

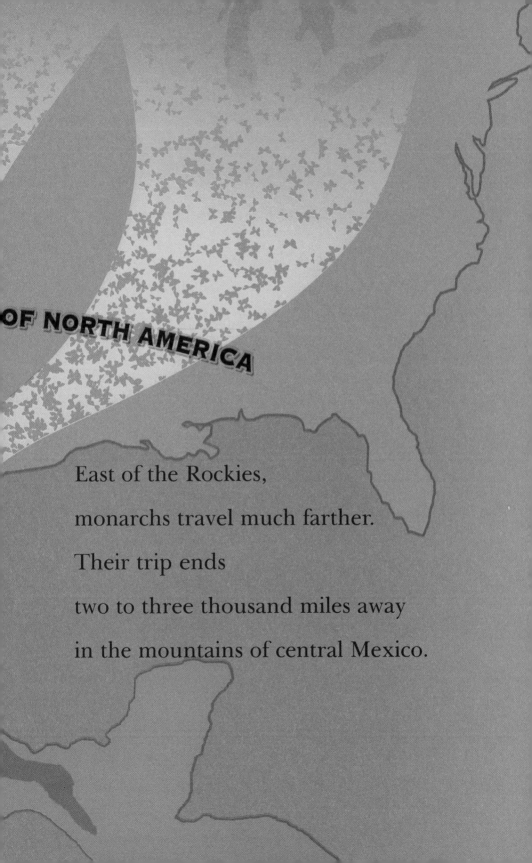

OF NORTH AMERICA

East of the Rockies,

monarchs travel much farther.

Their trip ends

two to three thousand miles away

in the mountains of central Mexico.

Monarchs can't fly

for a long stretch of time.

Their orange and black wings

are frail and tear easily.

So how do they get

all the way

to Mexico?

Most of the time,

they glide

on gusts of warm winds.

They can glide

for miles and miles.

From time to time,

they make a stop.

They stop to drink water.

They also drink a sweet liquid
in the flowers.

It is called nectar.

Nectar gives the butterflies energy.

Butterflies do not have mouths.

Instead, there is a tube on their head.

It curls in and out and works like a straw.

It is called a proboscis

(say: pro-BOSK-kiss).

Zup! The butterflies sip up lots of nectar.

The butterflies

stop in a flower garden.

A cat is hiding nearby.

The cat is old and slow—

too slow to catch birds.

But it can still catch butterflies.

The cat watches and waits.

Then it springs.

Will it catch any butterflies?

No! The butterflies are lucky.

They fly up and away.

Mile after mile,

the monarchs travel south.

They travel by day.

They never fly at night.

It is too cold at night,

so they rest.

During heavy storms,

the monarchs find shelter.

In high winds,

they also find shelter.

But on sunny days,

they are on the move again.

They fly over water.

They fly above city streets.

They cross a desert.

As they get closer to Mexico,
groups of monarchs join up—
hundreds, then thousands,
then millions.
The last leg of the trip is over
the Sierra Madre Oriental
Mountains.

The butterflies spend

the winter in

the forests of Mexico.

None of the monarchs has ever

made the trip before.

So how did they know

where to go?

Maybe the curve of the earth

helped them.

Maybe the position of the sun

helped them.

Scientists do not know

for sure.

For a long time,

scientists did not even know

about the monarchs' trip!

They thought monarchs hid

in safe, warm places

during the winter.

Then, in the summer of 1975,

US scientists carefully put tiny stickers

on some monarchs.

The stickers were like ID tags.

Several weeks later,

these monarchs from the US

showed up in Mexico.

For the people of central Mexico,
the arrival of the monarchs
is a big event.

There are festivals.

Buses of tourists come

to see this amazing sight.

Everyone watches

clouds of butterflies

filling the sky.

They fly down, down, down.

They cling to the trunks and

branches of fir trees.

No needles can be seen—

only monarchs!

It is a good place

to spend the winter.

It is not too hot

or too cold.

Most of the time,

the monarchs stay

in a light sleep.

On warmer days,

they may wake and fly

to find a little water.

Of course, there are dangers.

Some days do get too cold.

Butterflies on the outside

of clusters

freeze and die.

Other animals are a threat.

Black-eared mice like

to eat butterflies.

People are a danger, too.

They cut down the fir trees

and sell the logs.

The people need money.

But the butterflies need

the trees.

The trunks and branches
give off heat.
The heat keeps
the monarchs alive
until spring comes.

By March, it is time to begin

the trip home.

But first the monarchs mate.

Then they fly north—

just far enough north

to find milkweed plants.

The monarchs lay their eggs
on milkweed leaves.
The monarchs have been alive
for seven to nine months now.
That is a very long time
for a butterfly.
Now their life is over.
Their offspring will continue
the trip north.

Here you see the stages

from egg to caterpillar to chrysalis . . .

and finally to butterfly.

It takes about four weeks

for the eggs to turn

into butterflies.

These new monarchs live

for about a month.

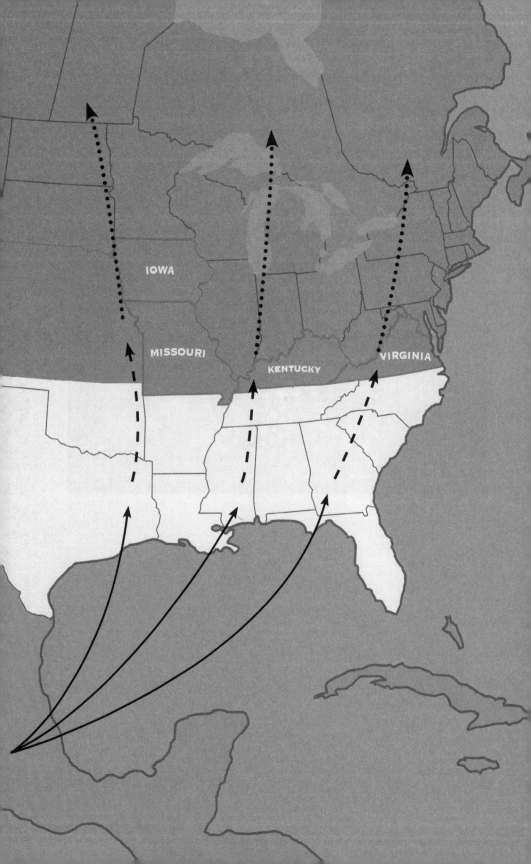

IOWA

MISSOURI

KENTUCKY

VIRGINIA

In a month,

they get as far

as the southern United States.

These are shown in yellow.

Their offspring continue

the journey.

In a month,

they reach states as far north

as Virginia, Missouri,

Kentucky, and Iowa.

These states are shown

in orange.

It is their offspring

that make

the last leg of the trip.

This area is shown in green.

It is summer by the time

the monarchs return

to the very same meadows

where the trip began

so long ago—

and where it will begin

all over again.